C000245396

Meet Jesus
with Pope Francis

by
Rev Nick Donnelly

*All booklets are published thanks to the
generous support of the members of the
Catholic Truth Society*

CATHOLIC TRUTH SOCIETY
PUBLISHERS TO THE HOLY SEE

Contents

Images: Page 4 *The Calling of St Matthew*, c. 1598-1601 (oilonpanel), Caravaggio, Michelangelo Merisi da (1571-1610)/Contarelli Chapel, S. Luigi dei Francesi, Rome, Italy/Bridgeman Images. Page 46 *Light of the World*, c.1851-53 (oil on canvas), Hunt, William Holman (1827-1910) /Keble College, Oxford, UK/By kind permission of the Warden and Fellows of Keble College, Oxford/Bridgeman Images.

ISBN 978 1 78469 040 3

Acknowledgements and thanks

This short book draws on a series of talks I gave during Our Lady of Furness' Parish Retreat held in October 2014 at the Monastery of Our Lady of Hyning, Warton, near Carnforth, Lancashire.

I would like to thank my fellow parishioners and members of other parishes in the Furness Deanery for their thoughtful and enthusiastic response during the retreat; the Bernardine sisters for their hospitality and warmth; Fr Manny Gribben for his encouragement and support, and Martina, my wife, for her invaluable partnership in my ministry.

I dedicate this book to Father Abbot and the Benedictine community of Buckfast Abbey in thanksgiving for their generous welcome to the School of the Annunciation.

The Calling of St Matthew by Michelangelo Merisi da Caravaggio,
Church of St Louis of France, Contarelli Chapel, Rome, 1599

Preface

Some years ago as a tourist in Rome, in the darkness of a church, I stood before Caravaggio's great painting, *The Calling of St Matthew*. I was waiting for someone else to pay for the lights to go on so I could see the painting.

It was before this very painting that Pope Francis experienced his conversion. Looking up at *St Matthew* his heart was filled with joy, knowing that he too was a sinner who has been saved by the mercy of God. Pope Francis observed Matthew's reluctance to let go of his money:

> That finger of Jesus, pointing at Matthew. That's me. I feel like him. Like Matthew. It is the gesture of Matthew that strikes me: he holds on to his money as if to say, "No, not me! No, this money is mine." Here, this is me, a sinner on whom the Lord has turned his gaze.

This made me realise with a shock that just like Matthew I was a sinner, preferring to stay in the dark because I didn't want to let go of my money. Pope Francis has helped me see the freedom and joy to be gained by following his example. I too can honestly admit "I am a sinner." There is a joy in realising who I really am because, like Matthew, I know with certainty that Our Lord loves me and calls me to walk out of the darkness into his glorious light.

Listening to Pope Francis's words about how our lives will change if we have a real encounter with Jesus can be exciting, challenging and disturbing. If you listen, and follow his advice, you will not be the same person you were before you heard him. Wonderful things will happen in your life if you take to heart what Pope Francis wants to tell you about how to get close to Christ.

May God keep you and may you find joy in the love of Christ.

Deacon Nick Donnelly,
Our Lady of Furness, Barrow, Cumbria

The Joy of Encountering Jesus

Pope Francis knows that we are often restless and dissatisfied about ourselves and the state of the world. He wants us to understand the underlying cause of this restlessness which often leaves us feeling frustrated and unfulfilled. To this end, he tells the story of a young man who was brought up a Catholic but left the Church because he failed to "find the answer to his questions, to his heart's desires, and was attracted by other proposals." Pope Francis relates how the young man studied, had fun, experienced intense friendships, intense love, embarked on a brilliant career, but remained restless. The Holy Father explains:

> But in his heart, there remained the restlessness of the search for the profound meaning of life. His heart was not asleep; it was not anaesthetised by success, by things, by power. And he discovered that God was waiting for him and, in fact, never stopped looking for him first.[1]

The young man was St Augustine of Hippo, who wrote the following about his experience of restlessness: "you have made us for yourself, and our heart is restless until it rests in you."[2] St Augustine came to understand that the origin of his restlessness was the desire for God that is at the heart of every person. As the *Catechism of the Catholic Church* (*CCC*) explains:

> The desire for God is written in the human heart, because man is created by God and for God; and God never ceases to draw man to himself. Only in God will he find the truth and happiness he never stops searching for (*CCC* 27).

The purpose of our lives

Pope Francis wants us to understand that the main purpose of our lives is personally to encounter Jesus Christ. He sees the life of St Augustine as pointing us to that truth:

> In Augustine, there is this restlessness of the heart that leads him to the personal encounter with Christ, it leads him to understand that God that he searched for far from himself, is the God close to every human being, the God close to our heart, more intimate to us than ourselves.

Pope Francis is also concerned that Christians often miss out on the whole purpose of our lives because we make the mistake of assuming that we'll only meet Jesus when we die. He says: "We can ask ourselves this question: When will we meet Jesus - only at the end? No, no, no!"[3]

Every day is an opportunity for us to encounter the person of Jesus Christ if we have the expectation that we'll meet him. All it takes, according to Pope Francis, is becoming more aware of the many ways Jesus is already close to us in our day-to-day lives:

> Our whole life is an encounter with Jesus: in prayer, when we go to Mass, and when we do good works, when we visit the sick, when we help the poor, when we think of others, when we are not selfish, when we are loving… in these things we always meet Jesus. And the journey of life is precisely this: journeying in order to meet Jesus.[4]

What does Pope Francis mean by "encounter Jesus"?

Both Pope Francis and Pope Benedict teach about the necessity of each one of us "encountering" Christ. Pope Benedict describes this encounter with Christ as being absolutely essential to being truly Christian:

> We are only Christians if we encounter Christ. Of course, he does not show himself to us in this overwhelming, luminous way, as he did to Paul to make him the Apostle to all peoples. But we too can encounter Christ in reading Sacred Scripture, in prayer, in the liturgical life of the Church. We can touch Christ's Heart and feel him touching ours. Only in this personal relationship with Christ, only in this encounter with the Risen One do we truly become Christians.[5]

Pope Francis also believes that this "encounter" is essential to our lives and he has talked and written about it many times since becoming pope. In the first sentence of the Pope's Apostolic Exhortation, *Evangelii Gaudium*, he says, "The joy of the gospel fills the hearts and lives of all who encounter Jesus." And he's also said:

> The encounter with the living Jesus, in the great family that is the Church, fills the heart with joy, because it fills it with true life, a profound goodness that does not pass away or decay.[6]

Why do both popes use the word "encounter"? Why not "meet" Jesus? Why not "hear" Jesus? 'Encounter' is a very strong word, describing a very definite event. The word 'encounter' comes from an Old French word meaning 'come up against', as two armies might come up against each other in battle. Two armies encounter each other.

At first sight this seems a strange word to use about Jesus in our lives. To me the word 'encounter' conveys the sense that if we truly meet Jesus he'll turn our lives upside down, he will overpower us with his love and his truth.

Change perspective

I have met Catholics who have told me that they've never "met Jesus", that they've never "experienced" the presence of Jesus in their lives. This is really sad. What Pope Francis is saying is that if you change your perspective from hoping that you will only meet Jesus in heaven, to assuming that you will meet Jesus everyday, it will revolutionise your Christian life.

To achieve this change in perspective, it helps to know two fundamental principles of Catholic sacramental life and prayer:

1) *Jesus's presence continues through his sacraments*

It's a basic principle of sacramental theology that when you receive any of the sacraments it is Our Lord Jesus Christ who bestows them on you. It is Christ who baptised you; it is Christ who confirmed you; it is Christ who gives himself to you in Holy Communion; it is Christ who forgives your sins.

Furthermore, through the activity of the Holy Spirit in Sacred Scripture and the sacraments we really enter into the drama of Christ's life. Our participation in the sacraments during the Church's liturgical year is not like watching an historical re-enactment, like modern day re-creations of historical events. Instead, the sacraments enable us to encounter the living presence of Our Lord - we kneel with the shepherds and Magi before the manger of Bethlehem, we are plunged into the Jordan by John the Baptist, we stand with the women as they witness Jesus's death on the cross, we wait with Mary and the apostles for the coming of the Holy Spirit.

It is not merely a commemoration of the events of the Gospel or other events in the Church's life, in an artistic form. It is also an actualisation of these facts, their

renewal upon earth. The Christmas service does not
merely commemorate the birth of Christ. In it Christ
is truly born in a mystery, as at Easter he rises again.
So with the Transfiguration, the entry into Jerusalem,
the mystery of the Last Supper, the passion, burial and
ascension of Christ…The life of the Church in her
liturgy discloses to our senses the continuing mystery
of the Incarnation. (Sergei Bulgakov[7])

2) God has sent his Holy Spirit into your heart

The Holy Spirit dwells in your heart - whether you know
it or not - through the sanctifying grace you received
through the sacrament of Baptism and if you remain free
from mortal sin. Pope Francis wants you to realise that this
presence of the Holy Spirit in your heart is the single most
important fact of your life:

How could we do without the Holy Spirit! Every
Christian in his or her life requires a heart open to the
sanctifying action of the Holy Spirit. The Spirit, promised
by the Father, is he who reveals Jesus Christ to us, but
who makes us…gives us the possibility to say: Jesus!
Without the Spirit, we could not say this. He reveals
Jesus Christ, who leads us to a personal encounter with
him, and who, in so doing, changes our life. A question:
is this your experience? Share it with others! In order to
share this experience, you must live it and witness to it![8]

At first sight Pope Francis's admission that we cannot say the name of Jesus without the Holy Spirit may seem strange. But what he means is that we cannot say the name of Jesus as a prayer to the Father without the Holy Spirit. As St Paul puts it:

> "The Spirit too comes to help us in our weakness. For when we cannot choose words in order to pray properly, the Spirit himself expresses our plea in a way that could never be put into words." (*Rm* 8:26). "…because the proof that you are sons is that God has sent the Spirit of his Son into our hearts: the Spirit that cries, 'Abba! Father!'" (*Ga* 4:6).

Pope Francis knows for certain that we'll personally encounter Jesus if we expect to meet Jesus through his sacraments and through the presence of the Holy Spirit. We just have to be open to the possibility.

Am I too great a sinner to encounter Jesus?

Pope Francis mentions that when he tells people they can encounter the person of Jesus in this life, some doubt him saying, "but Father, you know that for me, this journey, it's a brutal journey. I'm a great sinner. I've committed many sins. How can I meet Jesus?"[9]

If we fear we are too great a sinner to encounter Jesus, Pope Francis wants to reassure us that we can meet Our Lord through the sacrament of confession:

You know that the people Jesus sought out the most were the biggest sinners. Although many would reproach Jesus for this, Christ would say "I came for the sinners who need healing." Jesus sees our sins. And in our journey - ours, we're all sinners, all of us - when we make mistakes, when we sin, Jesus comes even then, and he forgives us. And this forgiveness that we receive in confession is a meeting with Jesus.

Pope Francis: our lives are a journey

Pope Francis sets our encounter with Christ in the context of our lives seen as a journey. This is a common image in Christianity. In the Old Testament, the dominant image of journey is the Exodus of the tribes from slavery in Egypt to encounter the Lord on Sinai and on into the Promised Land. In the New Testament, the Gospels set their account of Our Lord's life in the context of a number of journeys, and especially his journey with the apostles from Galilee in the north to Jerusalem in the south.

But in his unique way, Pope Francis has introduced new ways of reflecting on our lives as a journey. He asks us to consider if we have come to a standstill on our journey or if we have taken the wrong road, or most dangerous of all, whether we have become "spiritual tourists":

There is another, even more dangerous group, because they deceive themselves. They journey but make no headway. There are wandering Christians: they go round and round as though life were an existential tour with no goal and end…they do not take the promises seriously. They go round and round and deceive themselves for they say: "I am walking." No; you are not walking, you are wandering! The Lord asks us not to stop, not to take the wrong road and not to wander through life. He asks us to look to the promises, to go forward with the promises before us, like the man from the Gospel of John, who "believed in Jesus' promises and took to the road." It is faith which enables us to set out and continue on the journey.[10]

The crucial attitude to have, according to Pope Francis, is one of attentiveness to the fact that we are on a journey. A journey has a start, an origin, and a journey ends at a destination.

The origin of your journey

Where and when did your journey start? Some people reply that their journey began with their conception, or their birth, or their baptism or during a moment of profound conversion. These are all essential stages in our journey but I would like you to reflect on the revealed truth that your journey began before your conception and birth.

The Bible tells us that our journey began before the creation of the universe. The Lord's word to Jeremiah equally applies to each one of us, "before I formed you in the womb I knew you" (*Jr* 1:4). The same truth is revealed in St Paul's Letter to the Ephesians:

> Before the world was made, he chose us, chose us in Christ to be holy and spotless, and to live through love in his presence, determining that we should become his adopted sons, through Jesus Christ for his own kind purposes (*Ep* 1:4-5).

The origin of your journey through life is in the will of God, the choice of God, before the foundation of the universe. Before you were conceived and born, you were a cherished thought in the eternal mind of God. Our journey through life has a purpose and a direction given by God. As Pope Benedict puts it, "We are not some casual and meaningless product of evolution. Each of us is the result of a thought of God. Each of us is willed, each of us is loved, each of us is necessary."[11]

Pope Francis concludes from this that God has a plan for each one of us, and asks

> Do we let God write our lives? Or do we want to do the writing ourselves? Are we fleeing from God's plan for our lives? You can flee from God, being Christian, being Catholic…being a priest, bishop, Pope…we all, we all are able to flee from God. It is a daily temptation. To not listen to God, not listen to his voice, not hear in one's heart his proposal, his invitation.[12]

The destination of your journey

In the Middle Ages the journey of the Christian was known as "Leaving and Returning to God." We come from God as our Creator, the beginning of all things, and we will return to God, the consummation and end of all things. Pope Francis has shared with us his opinion that some of the most beautiful words in Scripture are these from St Paul's First Letter to the Thessalonians, "So we shall stay with the Lord for ever" (*1 Th* 4:17). The Holy Father reflects on the profound significance of these words for our lives using St John's image of "the new Jerusalem, coming down from God out of heaven, as beautiful as a bride all dressed for her husband" (*Rv* 21:2):

That is what awaits us! This, then, is who the Church is: she is the People of God who follows the Lord Jesus and who prepares herself day by day for the meeting with him, as a bride with her bridegroom. And this is not just an expression: there will be actual nuptials! Yes, because Christ, by becoming a man like us and making us all one with him, with his death and his Resurrection, truly wedded us and constituted us, as a people, his bride. This is none other than the fulfilment of the plan of communion and of love woven by God throughout history, the history of the People of God and also the very history of each one of us. It is the Lord who is in the lead.[13]

Furthermore, during the Middle Ages Christians understood that the purpose of the incarnation of the Son of God,
when God assumed a physical human nature, was to help
us return to God through the graces we receive through the
physical sacraments. The sacraments were given us by Our
Lord to help us reach our final destination.

All of the sacraments give us the graces necessary to
return to God: we are baptised and confirmed into the divine
life of God; we are healed of our sins through confession and
the sacrament of the sick; we are nourished and energised
with the Real Presence of Jesus in the Blessed Sacrament,
and many of us live our vocations and missions through
marriage and Holy Orders. God so wants us to return to
him, he has provided special graces to help us survive and
persevere until the end of the journey.

Pope Francis's prayer for a personal encounter with Jesus Christ

To help us encounter Christ anew through the journey of
our lives, Pope Francis invites us to pray for this each day:

I invite all Christians, everywhere, at this very moment,
to a renewed personal encounter with Jesus Christ, or at
least an openness to letting him encounter them; I ask
all of you to do this unfailingly each day. No one should
think that this invitation is not meant for him or her,
since "no one is excluded from the joy brought by the
Lord." The Lord does not disappoint those who take this

risk; whenever we take a step towards Jesus, we come to realise that he is already there, waiting for us with open arms. Now is the time to say to Jesus: "Lord, I have let myself be deceived; in a thousand ways I have shunned your love, yet here I am once more, to renew my covenant with you. I need you. Save me once again, Lord, take me once more into your redeeming embrace."[14]

Encountering Christ - some questions to ask ourselves

- How can I enjoy every day as an opportunity to encounter the person of Jesus Christ?
- How can I live in the joyful expectation that I will meet him?
- How can I share the joy of the Holy Spirit with others?
- How can I live and witness to my joy in the Holy Spirit?
- How can my faith enable me to set out and continue on the journey to God?
- How can I listen to God's voice and follow his plan for my life?

Lord, I have let myself be deceived;
in a thousand ways I have shunned your love,
yet here I am once more, to renew my covenant with you.
I need you.
Save me once again,
Lord, take me once more into your redeeming embrace.
(Pope Francis)

Seeking the Face of Our Lord Jesus Christ

Of you my heart has spoken: "Seek his face". It is your face, O Lord, that I seek; hide not your face. Instruct me, Lord, in your way. (Ps 26: 8-9,11).

This psalm expresses the deepest desire of our hearts: "It is your face, O Lord, that I seek; hide not your face." All of us are seeking the face of Jesus. Maybe there have been times in your life when you glimpsed the face of Our Lord, when he was close to you, when he guided you, when your day to day life was filled with the presence of Our Lord?

During those time our hearts became "little heavens" when we experienced a joy similar to that felt by the two disciples on the road to Emmaus when they encountered the Resurrected Lord, "They said to each other, 'Did not our hearts burn within us while he talked to us on the road and explained the scriptures to us?'" (*Lk* 24: 32).

When God hides his face

Maybe there have been times when he has hidden his face from you. Sometimes it seems that Our Lord hides his face when we most need him. And we ask the questions: where are you, God? Why are you so silent? Do you really exist or are you just make-believe?

Some of the most insistent cries in the Old Testament are Israel's desperate questions: where are you, Lord? Have you abandoned us, God? Why do you hide your face? "Lord, why do you stand afar off and hide yourself in times of distress?" (*Ps* 9:1).

During the times when God has seemed absent in my life, such as when my two children died, I have asked the same anguished questions. I saw a grief counsellor, I sought the guidance of spiritual directors, but when all is said and done what helped was praying before statues and images of the Crucified Christ. Pope Francis offers this advice when God seems absent:

> People who are living in difficult, sorrowful situations, who have lost so much or who feel alone and abandoned and come to complain and to ask these questions: why? They rebel against God. Continue to pray in this way, because this too is a prayer. As was that of Jesus, when he asked the Father: "why have you abandoned me?" Because to pray is to become truthful before God. One prays with reality. True prayer comes from the heart, from the moment that one is living. It is prayer in moments of darkness, in the moments of life where there is no hope.[15]

The Pope also offers two further pieces of advice for these times:

> Prepare yourself, for when darkness comes. Darkness will come, perhaps not as it did to Job, perhaps not as

difficult, but we will have a time of darkness. Everyone will. This is why it is necessary to prepare the heart for that moment. Pray, as the Church prays, with the Church, for so many brothers and sisters who suffer being outcast from themselves, in darkness and in suffering, with no hope at hand.[16]

Where do we seek for the face of Jesus?

I know that some Catholics, who are fit and well, say that they don't need to attend Mass because they can pray at home. There are also others who say that they don't need to go to confession because they can ask for God's forgiveness without the assistance of a priest. Pope Francis is certain that we can't find Jesus outside the Church as "Do-It-Yourself" Christians:

At times one hears someone say: "I believe in God, I believe in Jesus, but I don't care about the Church…" How many times have we heard this? And this is not good. There are those who believe they can maintain a personal, direct and immediate relationship with Jesus Christ outside the communion and the mediation of the Church. These are dangerous and harmful temptations. On the contrary, you cannot love God without loving your brothers, you cannot love God outside of the Church; you cannot be in communion with God without being so in the Church, and we cannot be good Christians if we are not together with those who seek to follow the Lord Jesus, as one single people, one single body, and this is the Church.[17]

Pope Francis on meeting Jesus

As I have said, Pope Francis uses the image of a journey to talk about the Christian life. The Holy Father tells us that the motivation of our journey should be the expectation to meet Our Lord. He says:

> We travel down this path to meet the Lord. We journey to meet him, to encounter him with our hearts and our lives, to meet him, the living One, as he is; to meet him in faith.[18]

Pope Francis talks about our meeting Jesus in his reflection on the Roman centurion meeting Our Lord as recounted in St Matthew's Gospel:

> When he went into Capernaum a centurion came up and pleaded with him. "Sir," he said "my servant is lying at home paralysed, and in great pain." "I will come myself and cure him" said Jesus. The centurion replied, "Sir, I am not worthy to have you under my roof; just give the word and my servant will be cured. For I am under authority myself, and have soldiers under me; and I say to one man: Go, and he goes; to another: Come here, and he comes; to my servant: Do this, and he does it." When Jesus heard this he was astonished and said to those following him, "I tell you solemnly, nowhere in

Israel have I found faith like this. And I tell you that
many will come from east and west to take their places
with Abraham and Isaac and Jacob at the feast in the
kingdom of heaven; but the subjects of the kingdom
will be turned out into the dark, where there will be
weeping and grinding of teeth." And to the centurion
Jesus said, "Go back, then; you have believed, so let
this be done for you." And the servant was cured at that
moment. (*Mt* 8:5-13).

The Pope concludes that the centurion encountered Jesus
and most importantly allowed Jesus to encounter him:

The Lord marvelled at the centurion. He marvelled at his
faith. The centurion made a journey to meet the Lord,
but he made it in faith. He not only encountered the
Lord, but he came to know the joy of being encountered
by him. And this is precisely the sort of encounter we
desire, the encounter of faith. To encounter the Lord,
but also to allow ourselves to be encountered by him.
This is very important.[19]

Why are we seeking Jesus?

Francis wants us to consider the real reasons why we are
seeking Jesus. Are we seeking Jesus because we are drawn
to his power: his power to heal; his power to forgive; his
power to explain? Are we seeking Jesus because we are
curious? Are we seeking Jesus because we desire beauty,

truth, goodness? These are all perfectly good reasons to want to meet Jesus. But the question Francis wants us to consider is, are we seeking Jesus only on our own terms? We seek Jesus, we desire to meet him, but do we want him to find us, to know us as we really are?

When we seek to meet Jesus only on our own terms Pope Francis describes us as wanting to be "masters of the moment." We want to be in control of meeting Jesus, we want to be masters of the moment. But if we want to truly encounter Jesus, we have to meet him on his terms, we have to let him be the master of the moment. Pope Francis says:

> When we allow ourselves to be encountered by him, he enters into us and renews us from within. This is what it means for Christ to come: to renew all things, to renew hearts, souls, lives, hope and the journey.[20]

Let down your defences and allow Jesus to be Lord

Pope Francis wants us to understand that we have to let our defences down if we want to truly meet Jesus. We have to "open our minds and hearts to him because when he comes to me, he may tell me what he wants me to do, which is not always what I want him to tell me."[21]

The Holy Father wants you to consider this question: do you ask the Lord what he intends for you in your life, or do you tell the Lord what you want him to do for you? It is important we never forget that "he is the Lord and he will tell me what he intends for me."

Pope Francis says wonderful things will happen if we never forget that Jesus is our Lord:

> The Lord does not look upon us all at once, as a mass of people: no, no! He looks at us one by one, in the face, in the eyes, for true love is not something abstract but rather something very concrete. Person to person. The Lord, who is a Person, looking at me, a person. That is why allowing the Lord to come and meet me also means allowing him to love me.[22]

Who is the Lord who seeks us?

Throughout his homilies and writings, Pope Francis always emphasises the importance of the Crucified Christ in our lives. He goes so far to say that if the Crucified Christ is not in our lives then we're not really Christians. This is the paradox of Pope Francis, by which I mean he appears to hold together two opposing or contradictory truths - Francis is the Pope of the Crucified Christ and Francis is the Pope of Joy! Not only does he not see this as a contradiction, Pope Francis says that we will only find true joy if the Crucified Christ is the centre and foundation of our lives.

Pope Francis on the Crucified Christ

Pope Francis could have chosen to focus on Christ the teacher, or Christ the Good Shepherd, Christ the healer, the Resurrected Christ. But since becoming pope he has very definitely focused on the importance of Christ's Passion and death on the Cross to the daily living of our Christian lives.

In his very first homily as Pope, Francis reflected on this passage from St Mark's Gospel:

And he began to teach them that the Son of Man was destined to suffer grievously, to be rejected by the elders and the chief priests and the scribes, and to be put to death, and after three days to rise again; and he said all this quite openly. Then, taking him aside, Peter started to remonstrate with him. But, turning and seeing his disciples, he rebuked Peter and said to him, "Get behind me, Satan! Because the way you think is not God's way but man's." He called the people and his disciples to him and said, "If anyone wants to be a follower of mine, let him renounce himself and take up his cross and follow me." (*Mk* 8: 31-34).

The newly elected Pope Francis gave this reflection:

The same Peter who confessed Jesus Christ, says, "You are the Christ, the Son of the living God. I will follow you, but let us not speak of the Cross. This has nothing to do with it." He says, "I'll follow you on other ways that do not include the Cross." When we walk without the Cross, when we build without the Cross, and when we profess Christ without the Cross, we are not disciples of the Lord. We are worldly, we are bishops, priests, cardinals, Popes, but not disciples of the Lord. I would like that all of us, after these days of grace, might have

the courage - the courage - to walk in the presence of the
Lord, with the Cross of the Lord: to build the Church on
the Blood of the Lord, which is shed on the Cross, and
to profess the one glory, Christ Crucified. In this way,
the Church will go forward.[23]

Pope Francis wants each one of us to consider our
attitude to the Crucified Christ, "Do you want to follow
Christ, but without the Cross? Do you assume that you can
follow Christ some other way?"[24] Do we avoid thinking
about the Cross of Christ? Do we blank the Cross from our
lives preferring Jesus at Bethlehem, Jesus in Galilee, Jesus
on Easter Sunday, Jesus in glory in heaven?

Why do we want Christ without his Cross?

Pope Francis suggests that the reason why many Christians
want Jesus without his Cross is because we fear the Cross.
Do you remember Mel Gibson's film *The Passion of the
Christ*? Every Lent I promise myself I'll watch *The Passion
of the Christ* on Good Friday as an act of devotion. But I
haven't yet because I find it too harrowing, too upsetting
and too real. Pope Francis says we're frightened of the
Cross because the Cross is frightening. And the first step
in accepting the Cross is admitting that we're frightened
of it. Pope Francis says it's okay to admit that we're
frightened of the Cross. The truth is that even Jesus was
afraid of it:

He could not deceive himself. He knew. And so great was his fear that on the night of Holy Thursday he sweated blood. He even asked God: "Father, remove this cup from me." But, he added: "Thy will be done." And this is the difference.[25]

Pope Francis goes on to say that if you have accepted being a follower of Christ you have to face this fear of the Cross:

We're frightened to ask "what will happen to me? What will my cross be like?" We do not know, but there will be a cross, and we need to ask for the grace not to flee when it comes. Of course it scares us, but this is precisely where following Jesus takes us. Jesus's words to Peter come to mind: "Do you love me? Feed…Do you love me? Tend…Do you love me? Feed…(cf. *Jn* 21:15-19), and these were among his last words to him: "They will carry you where you do not wish to go." He was announcing the Cross.[26]

Why is the Cross of Christ so important?

A priority for Pope Francis is to remind us of the fundamental reality of Christian life, that "through his wounds you have been healed" (*1 P* 2:24). The wounds and blood of Christ are the sources of healing and mercy that will rejuvenate the life of the Church and the lives of each one of us.

Pope Francis is reminding us of one of the most important truths of the Christian spiritual life, that nothing better conveys the love of God for us than the passion and death of Jesus. As Thomas à Kempis expresses it in *The Imitation of Christ*, "rest in Christ's passion and live willingly in his holy wounds. You will gain marvellous strength and comfort in adversities."

This truth is also conveyed in the medieval prayer, *Anima Christi* (translated as the well-known hymn 'Soul of my Saviour'):

> Blood of my saviour, bathe me in thy tide, wash me with water gushing from thy side. Strength and protection may they passion be, O blessed Jesus hear and answer me; Deep in thy wounds Lord hide and shelter me, so shall I never, never part from thee.

Pope Francis knows that it is through the wounds of the Crucified Christ that we encounter the love of God. One of Francis's first acts as pope was to give a meditation on Italian television on the Shroud of Turin in which he encourages us to meditate on the image of the Crucified Christ:

> How is it that the faithful, like you, pause before this icon of a man scourged and crucified? This image, impressed upon the cloth, speaks to our heart and moves us to climb the hill of Calvary, to look upon the wood of the Cross, and to immerse ourselves in the eloquent silence of love.[27]

Encountering Christ - some more questions for us

- What are the real reasons I am seeking Jesus?
- How can I let Jesus enter into me and renew me from within - heart, soul, life and hope?
- How do I stop telling the Lord what I want him to do for me, and ask him what he intends for me?
- How do I allow the Lord to come to meet me, to love me, person to person?
- How do I have the courage to walk in the presence of the Lord, with the Cross of the Lord?
- How do I place the Crucified Christ at the centre of my life?

Blood of my saviour, bathe me in thy tide,
wash me with water gushing from thy side.
Strength and protection may thy passion be,
O blessed Jesus, hear and answer me;
Deep in thy wounds, Lord, hide and shelter me,
so shall I never, never part from thee.
(Anima Christi)

The Joy of being Sinners
who have been Saved

In the previous chapter I wrote about Pope Francis being both the Pope of the Crucified Christ and the Pope of Joy. We looked at Pope Francis's understanding of the importance of placing the Crucified Christ at the centre of our lives as Christians.

In this chapter I want to tell you about Francis as the Pope of Joy, and how he holds both the Crucified Christ and an exuberant, life-enriching joy together. This is the paradox at the heart of Francis's understanding of the Christian life.

The conversion of Pope Francis

The key to unlock the enigma about how Pope Francis holds together both the Crucified Christ and exuberant joy is his personal encounter with Jesus as a seventeen-year-old boy. This experience, the conversion of Pope Francis, occurred sixty years ago when he was staying in Rome. In 1953, on the Feast of St Matthew, the young Jorge Bergoglio experienced, in a very special way, the loving presence of God in his life and the truth that he was a sinner who has been saved. He recounts that, after making his confession, he felt his heart touched and sensed the descent of the Mercy of God, who called him with a gaze of tender love. He described his conversion in a newspaper interview. When he was asked: who is Jorge Mario Bergoglio, he replied:

> I do not know what might be the most fitting description …I am a sinner. This is the most accurate definition. It is not a figure of speech, a literary genre. I am a sinner. The best summary, the one that comes more from the inside and I feel most true is this: I am a sinner whom the Lord has looked upon. I am one who is looked upon by the Lord.
>
> I do not know Rome well. I know a few things. These include the Basilica of St Mary Major; I always used to go there. I know St Mary Major, St Peter's…but when I had to come to Rome, I always stayed in Via della Scrofa. From there I often visited the Church of St Louis of France, and I went there to contemplate the painting of *The Calling of St Matthew* by Caravaggio. That finger of Jesus, pointing at Matthew. That's me. I feel like him. Like Matthew. It is the gesture of Matthew that strikes me: he holds on to his money as if to say, "No, not me! No, this money is mine." Here, this is me, a sinner on whom the Lord has turned his gaze. And this is what I said when they asked me if I would accept my election as pontiff. I am a sinner, but I trust in the infinite mercy and patience of our Lord Jesus Christ, and I accept in a spirit of penance.[28]

The conversion of St Matthew

Here is the passage from St Matthew's Gospel, written by St Matthew about his first encounter with Our Lord Jesus Christ:

> As Jesus was walking on from there he saw a man named Matthew sitting by the customs house, and he said to him, "Follow me." And he got up and followed him. While he was at dinner in the house it happened that a number of tax collectors and sinners came to sit at the table with Jesus and his disciples. When the Pharisees saw this, they said to his disciples, "Why does your master eat with tax collectors and sinners?" When he heard this he replied, "It is not the healthy who need the doctor, but the sick. Go and learn the meaning of the words: What I want is mercy, not sacrifice. And indeed I did not come to call the virtuous, but sinners." (*Mt* 9:9-13)

Four months after becoming Pope, Francis talked about the importance of remembering our first encounter with Christ, which he set in the context of the Gospel account of St Matthew's conversion. He asked the congregation to remember their first encounter with Christ, clearly referring to his own first encounter with Jesus:

> Remember always, it is like blowing on the embers of that memory, no? Blowing to keep the fire alive, always. That memory gives Matthew strength and to all of them to forge ahead: "the Lord has changed my life, I met the

Lord!" The taxpayers were sinners twice over, because they were attached to money and were also traitors to their country in the sense that they collected taxes from their own people for the Romans. Matthew feels Jesus's gaze upon him and he feels stunned. He hears Jesus's invitation, "follow me, follow me." Matthew is then full of joy but he's also doubtful because he's also very attached to money. It just took a moment and we see how Caravaggio was able to capture it, that man who was looking, but also, with his hands, was taking the money. There is a moment in which Matthew says yes, leaves everything and goes with the Lord. It is the moment of mercy received and accepted, "yes, I'm coming with you!" and it is the first moment of the meeting, a profound spiritual experience.[29]

What does it mean to be a sinner?

Pope Francis asks each one of us: how do you answer the question, who are you? Do you see yourself as a sinner? Do you see yourself as a sinner who has been saved? But to answer his questions honestly, we first need to know what it means to be a sinner.

On the plane trip back from World Youth Day in 2013 Pope Francis told journalists:

> If a person, whether it be a lay person, a priest or a religious sister, commits a sin and then converts, the Lord forgives, and when the Lord forgives, the Lord

forgets and this is very important for our lives. This is important: a theology of sin. Many times I think of St Peter. He committed one of the worst sins: that is, he denied Christ, and even with this sin they made him Pope. We have to think a great deal about that.[30]

But what is sin? Our generation, unlike other generations, has great trouble answering this question. One of the tragedies of the modern Church is that fewer and fewer Catholics receive the sacrament of confession. Why is this? Pope Benedict XVI says that "sin-repentance-penance" are the new taboos in modern culture.

How does Pope Francis describe sin?

For Pope Francis, being in a state of sin means being the opposite of God. Rightly, his definition of sin doesn't start from the nature of sin, but from the opposite of sin, the nature of God. This passage from First Letter of St John is his starting point in talking about God and our sin:

This is what we have heard from him, and the message that we are announcing to you: God is light; there is no darkness in him at all. If we say that we are in union with God while we are living in darkness, we are lying because we are not living the truth. *(1 Jn* 1:5-6).

Pope Francis describes sin as walking in darkness:

Walking in darkness means being overly pleased with

ourselves, believing that we do not need salvation. That is darkness! When we continue on this road of darkness, it is not easy to turn back. Therefore, John continues "If we say we are without sin, we deceive ourselves and the truth is not in us."[31]

The Holy Father concludes:

Look to your sins, to our sins, we are all sinners, all of us…This is the starting point.

During his first Christmas homily Pope Francis talked about our lives being an admixture of light and dark:

In our personal history too, there are both bright and dark moments, lights and shadows. If we love God and our brothers and sisters, we walk in the light; but if our heart is closed, if we are dominated by pride, deceit, self-seeking, then darkness falls within us and around us. "Whoever hates his brother - writes the Apostle John - is in the darkness; he walks in the darkness, and does not know the way to go, because the darkness has blinded his eyes." (*1 Jn* 2:11)[32]

The darkness of personal sin

What does Francis mean when he says that we walk in the darkness when we sin? The Holy Father has been very specific about the types of sins that are most destructive to our lives, families and parishes:

Jealousy and envy

Pope Francis judges the sins of jealousy, envy, gossip and slander as clear signs of the influence of the devil in our lives:

> Jealousy and envy open the doors to every evil thing, causing strife even between believers.[33]

> The envious and jealous person is a bitter person, he doesn't sing, he doesn't praise, he doesn't know what joy is; he is always looking at what others have.[34]

Gossip and slander

Pope Francis has often said that the poison fruit of jealousy and envy is gossip:

> The second poison fruit of jealousy and envy is gossip. There are those who cannot bear for anyone else to have anything and so the solution is to put the other person down, so that I am a bit higher.[35]

> He warns that gossip is the enemy of gentleness and love.

> There are so many enemies of gentleness, aren't there? Starting with gossip. When people prefer to tell tales, to gossip about others, to give others a few blows.[36]

Idols

It is true that nowadays, to some extent, everyone, including our young people, feels attracted by the many idols which take the place of God and appear to offer hope: money, success, power, pleasure. Often a growing sense of loneliness and emptiness in the hearts of many people leads them to seek satisfaction in these ephemeral idols.[37]

The first step out of darkness

Pope Francis recalls St Paul's insight into personal sin, that when we walk in darkness we often do things that we don't really want to do:

> The fact is, I know of nothing good living in me - living, that is, in my unspiritual self - for though the will to do what is good is in me, the performance is not, with the result that instead of doing the good things I want to do, I carry out the sinful things I do not want. When I act against my will, then, it is not my true self doing it, but sin which lives in me. (*Rm* 7:18-20).

The Holy Father draws this conclusion from St Paul's public admission that he is a sinner:

> These thoughts and acts of darkness make us slaves, we need this interior liberation of the Lord. But more important here is that, to find the way out of the darkness, Paul confesses his sin to the community, his tendency to sin. He doesn't hide it.[38]

The first step in allowing Christ to free us from the darkness of sin is to be honest with ourselves and honest with others. First we need to admit to ourselves and others that we have an ingrained tendency to sin and then we must resolve to no longer hide the fact that we are sinners.

The joy of being prisoners released from the darkness

When we make this first step of being honest that we are sinners, we are like the Prodigal Son who admits to himself that he has been walking in darkness and turns around to return to his father:

> Then he came to his senses and said, "How many of my father's paid servants have more food than they want, and here am I dying of hunger! I will leave this place and go to my father and say: Father, I have sinned against heaven and against you; I no longer deserve to be called your son; treat me as one of your paid servants." So he left the place and went back to his father. While he was still a long way off, his father saw him and was moved with pity. He ran to the boy, clasped him in his arms and kissed him tenderly. Then his son said, "Father, I have sinned against heaven and against you. I no longer deserve to be called your son." But the father said to his servants, "Quick! Bring out the best robe and put it on him; put a ring on his finger and sandals on his feet. Bring the calf we have been fattening, and kill it; we are going to have a feast, a celebration, because this son of mine was dead and has come back to life; he was lost and is found." And they began to celebrate. (*Lk* 15:17-24).

Did you notice what happens when the father sees the son walking back home, out of the darkness of pagan lands? Instead of standing on his dignity as a father who has been wronged by his unfaithful son, the father runs towards the son and embraces him with joyous love. Pope Francis says that this is the joy we encounter when we admit we're sinners and we experience the mercy of God:

> But if we confess our sins, he is faithful, he is so just he forgives us our sins, cleansing us from all unrighteousness…The Lord who is so good, so faithful, so just that he forgives.[39]

Field hospital in the midst of a battlefield

Since the days of the first Christians, Jesus has been understood as the divine physician who came from heaven to heal us of the diseases, wounds and injuries of sin. This image of Jesus as doctor has its origins in his own description of his ministry, which Pope Francis often quotes:

> When the Pharisees saw this, they said to his disciples, "Why does your master eat with tax collectors and sinners?" When he heard this he replied, "It is not the healthy who need the doctor, but the sick. Go and learn the meaning of the words: *What I want is mercy, not sacrifice*. And indeed I did not come to call the virtuous, but sinners." (*Mt* 9:11-13).

Consequently, one of Pope Francis' favourite images of the Church is a field hospital in the midst of a battlefield where sinners receive God's medicine of mercy, forgiveness and love:

> I see clearly that the thing the church needs most today is the ability to heal wounds and to warm the hearts of the faithful; it needs nearness, proximity. I see the church as a field hospital after battle. It is useless to ask a seriously injured person if he has high cholesterol and about the level of his blood sugars! You have to heal his wounds. Then we can talk about everything else. Heal the wounds, heal the wounds…And you have to start from the ground up.[40]

Pope Francis explains that the reason for the Son of God's incarnation, his becoming man, was to be able to get close to us and touch us in order to heal us of our sins:

> God gets involved with our misery, he draws close to our wounds and he heals them with his hands; he became man in order to have hands with which to heal us. Jesus's work is personal: one man committed the sin, one man came to heal it, for God does not save us merely by decree or by law; he saves us with tenderness, he saves us with caresses, he saves us with his life given for us.[41]

Encountering Jesus through Confession

Pope Francis has spoken many times of the importance of the sacrament of confession, which he sees as a special way of encountering Jesus, healer of our sins:

> The Sacrament of Reconciliation is a sacrament of healing. When I go to confession, it is in order to be healed, to heal my soul, to heal my heart and to be healed of some wrongdoing. The biblical icon which best expresses them in their deep bond is the episode of the forgiving and healing of the paralytic, where the Lord Jesus is revealed at the same time as the physician of souls and of bodies (cf. *Mk* 2:1-12; *Mt* 9:1-8; *Lk* 5:17-26).[42]

But in order to help us truly encounter the healing power of Jesus, Pope Francis challenges the common misunderstanding that going to confession is like going to the dry cleaners. The Holy Father says that people often have this mechanical understanding of confession, "You go in the confessional. You confess your sins. You pray the 'I Confess'. The priest absolves you."[43] Pope Francis wants us to understand that receiving the sacrament of reconciliation is not something mechanical but is an encounter with the person of Our Lord Jesus Christ, "But Jesus in the confessional is not a dry cleaner: it is an encounter with Jesus, but with this Jesus who waits for us, who waits for us just as we are."[44]

Pope Francis's tough love about shame

Pope Francis knows that many adults find confession extremely difficult and taxing, and a moment of intense struggle, but he wants to encourage us to persevere. And he does this in a very challenging way. He wants us to get over our phobia of shame.

Shame, like sin and guilt, has become a taboo in our society. But Pope Francis knows that shame and guilt can be good for us if they are signs of a healthy spiritual immune system fighting the destructive presence of sin in our lives. Shame can be particularly helpful because it keeps us humble before God, and each other. Pope Francis says:

> Shame is a true Christian virtue, and even human…the ability to be ashamed. Don't be one of the "unashamed," because they are people who do not have the ability to be ashamed and to be ashamed is a virtue of the humble, of the man and the woman who are humble and childlike before God.[45]

Pope Francis knows that in order to progress on the Christian journey, and encounter Our Lord, we need the humility and meekness that come from the shame of being honest about our sins. He concludes:

> Humility and meekness are like the frame of a Christian life. A Christian must always be humble and meek. And Jesus waits for us to forgive us. We can ask him a

question: is going to confession like going to a torture session? No! It is going to praise God, because I, a sinner, have been saved by him. And is he waiting for me to beat me? No, with tenderness to forgive me. And if tomorrow I do the same? Go again, and go and go and go…He always waits for us. This tenderness of the Lord, this humility, this meekness.[46]

This is why we should have the joy of prisoners who have been released from the Death Row of sin into the freedom of God's love and mercy.

Encountering Christ - some more questions for us

- What is my first memory of meeting Jesus?
- How do I answer the question, who am I?
- How do I meet Jesus in the sacrament of confession?
- Do I have honest shame about my sins?
- How do I become humble and meek?
- How do I celebrate the joy of being a sinner who is saved?

Father, I have sinned against heaven and against you.
I no longer deserve to be called your son;
treat me as one of your paid servants…
this son of mine was dead and has come back to life;
he was lost and is found. (St Luke)

Light of the World, c.1851-53 by William Holman Hunt,
Keble College, Oxford, UK

Pope Francis' Top Tips for a Healthy Catholic Life

First: Make sure prayer is the first task of your life

Pope Francis says the first task of our lives is prayer:

> The most important task in life is to pray, not to pray with many words…but to pray with the heart for this prayer enables us to gaze upon the Lord, to listen to the Lord, and to ask the Lord for what we need. And we know that prayer can work miracles.[47]

What does Pope Francis mean by prayer? He says prayer is opening the heart to the Lord.

> Prayer is not a lot of words, like a parrot. We truly pray with our hearts: gazing on the Lord, hearing the Lord, asking the Lord.[48]

Do you know the famous painting by William Holman Hunt called *The Light of the World*? It shows Jesus standing in the twilight holding a torch and knocking at a door. It is inspired by this passage from the Book of Revelation:

> Look, I am standing at the door, knocking. If one of you hears me calling and opens the door, I will come in to share his meal, side by side with him. (*Rv* 3:20).

Pope Francis says that prayer is opening the door to the Lord, so that he can do something. If we close the door, God can do nothing. He takes as an example the Gospel account of Martha and Mary:

In the course of their journey he came to a village, and a woman named Martha welcomed him into her house. She had a sister called Mary, who sat down at the Lord's feet and listened to him speaking. Now Martha who was distracted with all the serving said, "Lord, do you not care that my sister is leaving me to do the serving all by myself? Please tell her to help me." But the Lord answered: "Martha, Martha," he said "you worry and fret about so many things, and yet few are needed, indeed only one. It is Mary who has chosen the better part; it is not to be taken from her." (*Lk* 10:38-42).

Pope Francis reflects:

To the eyes of Martha, this was time lost, it even seemed, perhaps, a bit of a fantasy: gazing upon the Lord as if she were a awestruck child. But who wants that? The Lord does. He wants us to gaze at him, to listen to him. This is the better part, because Mary heard the Lord and prayed with her heart. Let us think on this Mary who has chosen the better part, and makes us see the way, as the door is opened to the Lord.[49]

Why is prayer of the heart so important?

Prayer of the Heart is important because Our Lord has told us that he dwells within our hearts.

> If anyone loves me he will keep my word, and my Father will love him, and we shall come to him and make our home with him. (*Jn* 14:23)

> St Paul teaches in his letter to the Ephesians:

> Out of his infinite glory, may he give you the power through his Spirit for your hidden self to grow strong, so that Christ may live in your hearts through faith… planted in love and built on love. (*Ep* 3:16)

There are over a thousand references to the heart in the Bible; the *Catechism of the Catholic Church* expresses its importance as follows:

> The heart is the dwelling-place where I am, where I live; according to the Semitic or Biblical expression, the heart is the place "to which I withdraw." The heart is our hidden centre, beyond the grasp of our reason and of others; only the Spirit of God can fathom the human heart and know it fully. (*CCC* 2563)

Pope Francis wants you to realise that your heart is the "temple of God," the sacred space within yourself where you can encounter Our Lord.

Second: remember that Mary is your mother

The Holy Father knows from personal experience that devotion to Mary is essential to a healthy Christian life because Mary leads us to encounter Jesus, her divine son. He tells the following story:

> Pay attention to this: if you do not have a great relationship with the Virgin, you have something of an orphan in your heart. I remember, thirty years ago I was invited to a family of practising Catholics. The parents were both university professors. They were also catechists. They had many children. At the table, they began to talk about Jesus Christ, about whom they were enthusiastic, and they said, "Thank God, we have gotten past the stage of the Blessed Virgin." "Oh?" I said then. "Yes, we don't need her any more because we found Christ…" That hurt me. I did not understand it very well. This is not mature! Forgetting your mother is not good. A great relationship with the Blessed Virgin helps us to have a great relationship with the Church: they are both mothers. You know the text of St Isaac of Stella: what can be said of Mary can be said of the Church and also of our soul. All three are feminine, all three are mothers, and all three give life. Our relationship with the Virgin is the relationship of a child.[50]

Third: Finding the three doors to enter
the mystery of Jesus

Pope Francis teaches that there are three doors that we must enter in order to encounter Our Lord. We need all three doors in our lives if we are to meet Jesus.

The first door is prayer and study

Padre Pio (St Pio of Pietrelcina) wrote to one of his spiritual daughters, "By studying spiritual books, one seeks Jesus; by praying, one finds him." And Pope Francis advises that to progress in the Christian life we must combine spiritual study with prayer.

> You must realise that studying without prayers is no use. We must pray to Jesus to get to know him better. By studying and praying we get a bit closer…But we'll never know Jesus without praying. Never! Never![51]

Pope Francis recommends that during each day we ask ourselves, how is the door leading to prayer in my life?

The second door is celebrating Jesus

Pope Francis says prayer on its own is not enough; we need the joy of celebrating the sacraments. Celebrating Jesus through his sacraments is important for the wellbeing of our lives. The Holy Father explains:

> The sacraments give us life, they give us strength, they nourish us, they comfort us, they forge an alliance

with us, they give us a mission. Without celebrating the sacraments, we'll never get to know Jesus; and this celebration belongs to the Church.[52]

Pope Francis recommends that during each day we ask ourselves, how is the door leading to celebration, the sacraments, in my life?

The third door is imitating Jesus

It used to be understood that the Christian life meant being like Jesus, imitating how he lived, how he thought, how he loved others. One of the great classics of the Christian life is called *The Imitation of Christ*. A modern version of this imitation of Christ is the slogan 'WWJD?' - "What Would Jesus Do?"

But nowadays instead of imitating Christ, people often say "I'm only human" as if this were an excuse not to imitate Jesus. The impetus to imitate Jesus is a truth, highlighted by the Second Vatican Council and emphasised by Pope St John Paul II, that Jesus is the standard and measure of what it means to be truly human:

The truth is that only in the mystery of the incarnate Word does the mystery of man take on light. For Adam, the first man, was a figure of him who was to come, namely Christ the Lord. Christ, the final Adam, by the revelation of the mystery of the Father and his love, fully reveals man to man himself and makes his supreme calling clear. (*Gaudium et Spes*, 22)

Pope Francis is clear that if we want to encounter Jesus, we must imitate him. He is also worried that the Book of the Gospel is very dusty because it's never opened:

Take the Gospel and ask: what did he do? How was his life? What did he tell us? What did he teach us? And try to imitate him. Take the Book of the Gospel, open it and you will discover how to imitate Jesus![53]

Fourth: the importance of praying for others

Pope Francis says intercessory prayer is very important because it seeks the good of others. Intercessory prayer is not something we leave behind out of preference for more "advanced" forms of prayer. He points to St Paul as the model for intercessory prayer because St Paul's heart was full of people:

Let us peer for a moment into the heart of St Paul, to see what his prayer was like. It was full of people: "…I constantly pray with you in every one of my prayers for all of you…because I hold you in my heart" (*Ph* 1:4, 7). Here we see that intercessory prayer does not divert us from true contemplation, since authentic contemplation always has a place for others.[54]

He also wants us to notice that St Paul refers to his heart as the seat of intercessory prayer. Intercessory prayer is an expression of the love that is in our heart. Pope Francis asks, is your heart full of people?

The gratitude of a heart full of people

Pope Francis also encourages us to make gratitude our primary type of intercessory prayer, praying in gratitude to God for the people in our lives. As St Paul prays, "First, I thank my God through Jesus Christ for all of you" (*Rm* 1:8). Pope Francis thinks our lives should be ones of constant thankfulness: "I never stop thanking God for all the graces you have received through Jesus Christ" (*1 Co* 1:4); "I thank my God whenever I think of you" (*Ph* 1:3). Such intercessory prayer is an expression of the gratitude which flows from a heart attentive to others. But how can we make gratitude central to our lives if we're disappointed, angry, sad, depressed? Pope Francis says

> We must tell the truth: Christian life [is] not just one big party. Not at all! We cry, we cry so many times. When we are sick; when we have a problem with our son, in the family, with our daughter, or wife, or husband; when we see that our salary does not reach the end of the month and we have a sick child; when we see that we cannot pay the mortgage on the house and we must somehow survive…So many problems, we have so many. But Jesus tells us: "Do not be afraid!"

> However, in times of trial we do not see this. It is a joy that is purified by trials, our everyday trials: "your sorrow will turn to joy". But it's hard to go to a sick person who is suffering greatly and say: "Come on!

Come on! Tomorrow you will have joy!" No, you cannot say this! We have to help them feel what Jesus made us feel. When we are in the dark, we do not see anything, [say] "I know, Lord, that this sorrow will turn to joy. I do not know how, but I know it!" An act of faith in the Lord. An act of faith![55]

Fifth: Pope Francis's five finger prayer

This simple method of prayer has been attributed to Pope Francis, and has been associated with him since he was the Cardinal Archbishop of Buenos Aires, Argentina.

With your hands drawn together in prayer, using the fingers on your hand, start with the thumb and pray these intentions in this order:

The thumb is closest to you.

First, pray for those who are closest to you. Our family and friends are easiest to remember. To pray for our dear ones is a "sweet obligation."

Next comes the index finger.

The index finger is often used to point out the way or to direct others, so pray for those who have taught you, instructed you and advised you. They need the support and wisdom to show direction to others.

The following is the tallest, the forefinger.

This finger stands out above the others and reminds us of

our leaders, secular and religious, all who have authority. They need God's guidance.

The fourth finger is the ring finger.

This is our weakest finger, and reminds us to pray for the weakest, the sick or those bearing heavy burdens. They need your prayers.

And finally we have our smallest finger, the smallest of all.

Our little finger reminds us to pray for ourselves. Having prayed for the other four groups first, we will be able to see our own needs in their proper perspective, and in relation to other people in our lives. We will be able to pray for our own needs in a better way.[56]

Encountering Christ - some resolutions

- Make prayer the first task (and joy) of your life.
- Feel that Mary is your mother.
- Find the three doors to enter the mystery of Jesus.
  a. The First Door is prayer and study.
  b. The Second Door is celebrating Jesus.
  c. The Third Door is imitating Jesus.
- Pray for others.
- Use Pope Francis's five finger prayer.

As you close your hands together in prayer
The thumb is closest to you - pray for those who are
closest to you.
Next comes the index finger, often used to point out the
way - pray for those who have taught you, instructed you
and advised you.
The following is the tallest, the forefinger which stands
out above the others - pray for our leaders, secular and
religious, who have authority.
The fourth finger is the ring finger, our weakest finger -
to pray for the weakest, the sick or those bearing heavy
burdens.
And finally we have our smallest finger, the smallest of all
- pray for yourself.

Endnotes

[1] Homily at Mass of the 184th General Chapter of the Augustinians *http://w2.vatican.va/content/francesco/en/homilies/2013/documents/papa-francesco_20130828_capitolo-sant-agostino.html*

[2] Augustine, *Confessions* 1.1.1, quoted *Catechism of the Catholic Church*, 30

[3] Homily during Pastoral Visit to the Roman Parish of St Cyril of Alexandria. *http://w2.vatican.va/content/francesco/en/homilies/2013/documents/papa-francesco_20131201_parrocchia-san-cirillo-alessandrino.html*

[4] Ibid

[5] Pope Benedict XVI, General Audience Address, St Paul's Conversion, *http://www.vatican.va/holy_father/benedict_xvi/audiences/2008/documents/hf_ben-xvi_aud_20080903_en.html*

[6] Angelus Address, 4th August 2013 *http://www.news.va/en/news/pope-francis-our-encounter-with-jesus-fills-our-he*

[7] Quoted in Evelyn Underhill, *Worship*, p. 76

[8] Address to members of the Catholic Fraternity of Charismatic Covenant Communities and Fellowships *http://www.news.va/en/news/to-members-of-the-catholic-fraternity-of-charismat*

[9] Op cit

[10] Morning Meditation in the Chapel of the Domus Sanctae Marthae, 31st March 2014. *http://w2.vatican.va/content/francesco/en/cotidie/2014/documents/papa-francesco-cotidie_20140331_existential-tourists.html*

[11] Pope Benedict XVI, Homily at Beginning of the Petrine Ministry of the Bishop ofRome,*http://www.vatican.va/holy_father/benedict_xvi/homilies/2005/documents/hf_ben-xvi_hom_20050424_inizio-pontificato_en.html*

[12] Morning Meditation in the Chapel of the Domus Sanctae Marthae *http://w2.vatican.va/content/francesco/en/cotidie/2013/documents/papa-francesco-cotidie_20131007_fleeing-god.html*

[13]General Audience, 15th October 2014, *http://w2.vatican.va/content/francesco/en/audiences/2014/documents/papa-francesco_20141015_udienza-generale.html*

[14]*http://w2.vatican.va/content/francesco/en/apost_exhortations/documents/papa-francesco_esortazione-ap_20131124_evangelii-gaudium.html*

[15] Morning Meditation in the Chapel of the Domus Sanctae Marthae, 30th September 2014*http://w2.vatican.va/content/francesco/en/cotidie/2014/documents/papa-francesco-cotidie_20140930_prayers-in-the-darkness.html*

[16] Ibid

[17] General Audience, 25th June 2014. *http://w2.vatican.va/content/francesco/en/audiences/2014/documents/papa-francesco_20140625_udienza-generale.html*

[18] Morning Meditation in the Chapel of the Domus Sanctae Marthae, 2nd December 2013. *http://m2.vatican.va/content/francescomobile/en/cotidie/2013/documents/papa-francesco-cotidie_20131202_meeting-jesus.html*

[19, 20, 21, 22] Ibid

[23] 'Missa Pro Ecclesia' with the Cardinal Elector, 14th March 2013. *http://w2.vatican.va/content/francesco/en/homilies/2013/documents/papa-francesco_20130314_omelia-cardinali.html*

[24] Ibid

[25]Morning Meditation in the Chapel of the Domus Sanctae Marthae, 28th September 2013.*http://m2.vatican.va/content/francescomobile/en/cotidie/2013/documents/papa-francesco-cotidie_20130928_fear-cross.html*

[26] Ibid

[27]*http://www.thecatholicuniverse.com/pope-francis-hails-the-shroud-of-turin-1932*

[28] Antonio Spadaro, 'A Big Heart Open to God: The exclusive interview with Pope Francis.' *http://www.americamagazine.org/pope-interview*

29 Morning Meditation in the Chapel of the Domus Sanctae Marthae, 5th July 2013.*http://w2.vatican.va/content/francesco/en/cotidie/2013/documents/papa-francesco-cotidie_20130705_mercy-remembrance.html;http://www.catholicnewsagency.com/news/the-self-righteous-can-cook-in-their-own-stew-says-pope/*

30 Press Conference of Pope Francis during the Return Flight. 2013. *http://w2.vatican.va/content/francesco/en/speeches/2013/july/documents/papa-francesco_20130728_gmg-conferenza-stampa.html*

31 Morning Meditation in the Chapel of the Domus Sanctae Marthae, 29th April 2013. *http://w2.vatican.va/content/francesco/en/cotidie/2013/documents/papa-francesco-cotidie_20130429_blessed-shame.html*

32 Solemnity of the Nativity of the Lord, 24th December 2013. *http://w2.vatican.va/content/francesco/en/homilies/2013/documents/papa-francesco_20131224_omelia-natale.html*

33 Morning Meditation in the Chapel of the Domus Sanctae Marthae, 23rd January2014*http://w2.vatican.va/content/francesco/en/cotidie/2014/documents/papa-francesco-cotidie_20140123_hearts-free.html*

34, 35 Ibid

36 Morning Meditation in the Chapel of the Domus Sanctae Marthae, 9th April 2013 *http://m2.vatican.va/content/francescomobile/en/cotidie/2013/documents/papa-francesco-cotidie_20130409_temptation-gossip.html*

37 Holy Mass in the Basilica of the Shrine of Our Lady of the Conception ofAparecida,24thJuly2013.*http://w2.vatican.va/content/francesco/en/homilies/2013/documents/papa-francesco_20130724_gmg-omelia-aparecida.html*

38 Morning Meditation in the Chapel of the Domus Sanctae Marthae, 25th October2013.*http://w2.vatican.va/content/francesco/en/cotidie/2013/documents/papa-francesco-cotidie_20131025_grace-ashamed.html*

39 Morning Meditation in the Chapel of the Domus Sanctae Marthae, 29th April 2013. *http://w2.vatican.va/content/francesco/en/cotidie/2013/documents/papa-francesco-cotidie_20130429_blessed-shame.html*

40 Antonio Spadaro, 'A Big Heart Open to God: The exclusive interview with Pope Francis.' *http://www.americamagazine.org/pope-interview*

[41] Morning Meditation in the Chapel of the Domus Sanctae Marthae, 22nd October 2013. *http://w2.vatican.va/content/francesco/en/cotidie/2013/documents/papa-francesco-cotidie_20131022_contemplation.html*

[42] General Audience, 19th February 2014. *http://w2.vatican.va/content/francesco/en/audiences/2014/documents/papa-francesco_20140219_udienza-generale.html*

[43] Morning Meditation in the Chapel of the Domus Sanctae Marthae, 29th April 2013 *http://w2.vatican.va/content/francesco/en/cotidie/2013/documents/papa-francesco-cotidie_20130429_blessed-shame.html*

[44, 45, 46] Ibid

[47] Morning Meditation in the Chapel of the Domus Sanctae Marthae, 8th October 2013. *http://w2.vatican.va/content/francesco/en/cotidie/2013/documents/papa-francesco-cotidie_20131008_better-part.html*

[48, 49] Ibid

[50] Q&A With Seminarians in Rome, 12th May 2014. *http://www.zenit.org/en/articles/full-text-of-pope-francis-q-amp-a-with-seminarians-in-rome*

[51] Morning Meditation in the Chapel of the Domus Sanctae Marthae, 16th May 2014. *http://w2.vatican.va/content/francesco/en/cotidie/2014/documents/papa-francesco-cotidie_20140516_three-doors.html*

[52, 53] Ibid

[54] *http://w2.vatican.va/content/francesco/en/apost_exhortations/documents/ papa-francesco_esortazione-ap_20131124_evangelii-gaudium.html*

[55] Morning Meditation in the Chapel of the Domus Sanctae Marthae, 23rd May 2014. *http://w2.vatican.va/content/francesco/en/cotidie/2014/documents/papa-francesco-cotidie_20140523_sadness-joy.html;http://www.news.va/en/news/pope-at-mass-joy-in-hope*

[56] *http://www.obituariosdevenezuela.com/2013/03/conocian-la-oracion-de-los-cinco-dedos-famosisima-y-el-autor-es-el-papa-francisco/*

Who Is the Devil?
What Pope Francis says

Deacon Nick Donnelly

To the surprise of some, Pope Francis has devoted considerable energy in exhorting the faithful to take the devil seriously. In his homilies, speeches and writings he has made clear that while we need not be afraid of the devil, his activity today can be readily identified. The Christian's task is to unmask and counter this activity, with vigilance, prayer and mercy. Our Easter renewal of Baptismal promises is no theatre but involves a radical rejection of Satan and all his works and empty promises.

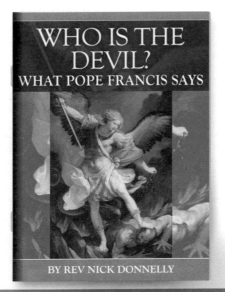

DO890   ISBN 978 1 86082 923 9

The Joy of the Gospel

Petroc Willey and Barbara Davies

This excellent guide, read alongside Pope Francis' *Evangelii Gaudium*, helps us to pray and meditate on its meaning in the light of Scripture and Tradition.

This meditative approach facilitates an encounter with Christ so that we are responsive to his call to ongoing conversion, and a deeper reception of his love. The Guide draws on Scripture, short references to the liturgy, the lives of the saints, papal teaching, and the Catechism.

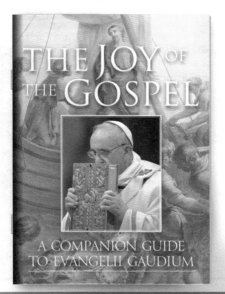

DO896 ISBN 978 1 78469 022 9

A world of Catholic reading at your fingertips...

Catholic Faith, Life & Truth for all